# LEARN TO LET GO

Leave your worries and stress behind

Health and Wellbeing  50MINUTES.com

# LEARN TO LET GO

Leave your worries and stress behind

Written by Elise Savaro
Translated by Rebecca Neal

Health and Wellbeing  50MINUTES.com

# LEARN TO LET GO

- **Problem:** while the idea of letting go is at the heart of many self-help books, it remains somewhat mysterious, and it is hard to know what we actually need to get rid of in order to live in the moment. Moreover, it is difficult to understand what living in the moment actually means.
- **Aim:** to realise that, while we cannot always change the course of events, we can adjust our outlook and the way we see things.
- **FAQs:**
  - Does everyone find it equally difficult to let go?
  - Do children find it easier to let go?
  - What makes it difficult for us to let go?
  - To what extent should we let go?
  - What is the best way to let go?

We hear about letting go all the time nowadays, but few of us really understand what it means. It is often presented as an obligation, an objective to reach and something that does not take much effort. Most of us will have been told to "just let it go" when we were worried or stressed. However, letting go is no mean feat when we find ourselves mired in problems.

The Swiss philosopher Alexandre Jollien invites us to "let go, even of letting of go[1]" (Petit traité de l'abandon, or "Little Treatise of Abandonment"); in other words, we should not consider letting go as a new constraint, but rather as an opportunity to relax by accepting certain unpleasant events or situations that are out of our control without blowing them out of proportion. However, this does not mean that we are adopting a defeatist or passive attitude – quite the opposite, in fact!

The story below, which is often used in psychology classes, will give you a better understanding of this concept:

> In Malaysia, there is a traditional monkey-hunting practice that involves cutting a coconut in half, scraping out the flesh and replacing it with a few grains of rice, before closing it again, leaving a small opening. The monkey is enticed by the coconut hanging from a tree and puts

---

1.  This quotation has been translated by 50Minutes.com.

its hand in it to get the rice. When the coconut closes again and traps it, it cries out and whimpers even though it could simply take its hand out and escape from the hunters. The monkey does not let go of the rice and save itself because it is too attached to its spoils. We do the same thing! Rather than taking a step back and putting things into perspective, we stubbornly cling to our thoughts.

The fact that we are thinking beings who tend to make things difficult for ourselves means that we have a lot more worries than monkeys, but it also means that we have the ability to observe ourselves and correct our behaviour, so that we are no longer guided by our reflexes.

This guide aims to give a more precise definition of the concept of letting go, introduce you to a range of techniques to help you to let go and help you to put these techniques in practice depending on your situation. It bears repeating once again that letting go does not mean giving in or accepting defeat, but is actually a way of improving your wellbeing!

# UNDERSTANDING HOW TO LET GO

## CONTROL AND ATTACHMENT: THE OPPOSITE OF LETTING GO

To understand the concept of letting go, we first need to consider its opposites, namely control and excessive attachment.

### Control

We use points of reference established from childhood onwards to adapt ourselves to the world. Our upbringing, environment and personality all shape our outlook on the world. This provides us with consistency and makes our interactions with our surroundings more or less harmonious. Controlling, or at least trying to control, a situation, reassures us. When we lose our grip on events, stress takes over us.

> "I call the crèche at least three times a day to reassure myself that everything is going well with Harry, and generally it is. The supervisors

tell me that there's no point calling and that it gets in the way of their work a bit, but I can't bring myself to go a whole day without reassuring myself that things are going well. If I don't call, I can't stop worrying." (Charlotte, 29, mother to a 6-month-old baby)

"I feel very uncomfortable on planes, even though I have to fly several times a month, mainly to Africa and Europe. I reassure myself by reading a little book that explains how planes work and the minimal risk I'm running the night before every flight. When I'm on the plane, I tend to watch everything, and as soon as I see something unusual I call a steward or hostess to ask them about it. That destresses me, and I feel as though I'm taking charge of the out-of-control plane, which is my biggest fear." (Michael, 42)

## Attachment

Attachment means granting importance to values, ideas, feelings, the elements in our environment and, of course, people. Our ego and personality make us believe that it would be very difficult to abandon these attachments, that we would be unhappy if we did not have them, or even that we could not live without them.

We must recognise that everything that has been a part of us since childhood is the material that we use to build ourselves, and it can therefore be used to change ourselves. The past inspires feelings of regret and nostalgia and, on a more harmful level, a great deal of suffering, anxiety and even depression.

As an example, we can consider the situation of the Inuits in Greenland, who have been undergoing major environmental and cultural changes (the spread of Western culture, the loss of their nomadic lifestyle, melting ice sheets and disruption to flora and fauna) for years. All these changes have resulted in the disappearance of the traditional, ancestral way of life that the indigenous inhabitants depended on for their mental and physical balance. Alcoholism, depression and obesity, which had never troubled the region before, have emerged as new public health problems. The suddenness of the cultural change did not give them time to take a step back, find new ways of living and therefore move past the feeling of loss.

Time also plays a vital role in the attachment process, because it helps to anchor people in their environment: the longer you stay in the same apartment, the more objects, furniture and memories you will accumulate and the harder it will be to move. You will be sad to leave the place that was the setting for so many experiences. You may also move because of a sudden negative event, such as a burglary, but this reaction is more like fleeing than letting go.

## Our brains: another obstacle to letting go

Our brain's natural function is to think. We are constantly thinking without even realising it, and when we reflect we sift through this jumble of thoughts. However, when our brain is put under too much pressure, it stops working as it should. This natural tendency is heightened in the modern world, as the internet, smartphones and other electronic devices attract our attention all day long and constantly take up space in our thoughts. These new instant sources of communication are an additional source of pressure in our already stressful daily lives. In addition, we are now facing information overload, which is not a good thing and gives us a very complex and often harsh outlook on the world. Besides this, as we get older, we take on more and more responsibilities: children, work, the challenges of stepfamilies, money worries, and so on.

This excess of responsibilities and information clutters up our brain, leaving it unable to work smoothly. We are overwhelmed, which makes it very difficult to let go. This is why it is so important to unburden ourselves, clear our minds and get back to the things that really matter. Our brains need calm and empty space to work – even if this empty space is an illusion, because our brains are always working.

We can start by calming all the noise and agitation that we can do without. For example, we could choose to stop responding to texts and emails as soon as we receive them. Similarly, we do not have to listen to the news every day. We need to begin by clearing out, as we cannot bring good things into our lives without first emptying our minds of everything that is weighing us down.

# Survival mechanisms

Control and attachment are two adaptation and survival mechanisms which, paradoxically, can also make us unhappy, imprison us and stop us from living life to the full.

If we have a very clearly defined vision of the world and do not want to change it because we think it represents an ideal, we will not adapt to life and will fail to embrace everything it can offer us. Life is complex and changeable, and it is truly important to be aware of this. Humans have known about this reality for many centuries thanks to the concept of impermanence, which appears in Eastern philosophy and has been observed in a slightly different form by many Western philosophers since Antiquity.



As an example, we can take the notion of impermanence as it appears in Buddhism, which, along with yoga, is the most popular Eastern philosophy in Europe. Impermanence, also known as Anitya, is one of the characteristics of all things: nothing is unchanging, and everything is born, evolves and ends up disappearing. This state of impermanence causes suffering (*dukkha*). Buddhism teaches that things that are impermanent are not satisfying and cause suffering, because we have a natural tendency to become attached to things. The bonds we form with the things and people around us reassure us and seem to fulfil us. However, somewhat paradoxically, this impermanence allows spiritual advancement. Impermanence and the resulting suffering allow us to become aware that our minds are very inconsistent and subject to our emotions. This awareness then drives us to improve ourselves.

The path to enlightenment involves stabilising our minds and detaching ourselves from our emotions. Meditation, which is the main way of reaching enlightenment, will allow our minds to resist suffering. The enlightened person becomes stable in an unstable world. However, stability requires us to accept this changing world.

In reality, we are born, become children, adolescents and adults, and then get old; we embark on new projects, meet new people and lose people. Some experiences are pleasant and support our development, while others seem unpleasant, unfair and completely useless, and we feel that they only make us go backwards.

Of course, it is possible to sort through all that to only keep the best experiences, but we can also tell ourselves that it is the sum of our experiences that makes us more human and empathetic. Empathy is a positive feeling, both for us and for other people. All humans can feel suffering and joy, and understanding this makes us empathetic and leads us to universal love and, consequently, a certain peace of mind.

## WHY IS IT SO DIFFICULT TO LET GO?

As we have seen, the main obstacles to letting go are disruptive emotions and thoughts, which stop us from living our lives in a more adapted, fluid way. Alongside this, some attachments can also cause us pain when the bond is broken, for example by:

- the loss of a loved one, whether following a death, a separation or moving away;
- the loss of a job;
- moving house;
- the decline of our youth, health, physical condition, and so on.

In these cases, it is particularly challenging for us to accept the situation as it is and acknowledge that we cannot change anything, no matter what we do.

This difficulty in letting go can also be seen in small everyday things that consume our energy, such as:

- stubbornly trying to find a solution to a problem that has been troubling us for a long time;
- worrying about things that are not fully under our control, such as our children's results at school;
- wanting other people to see us as perfect.

All these elements stop us from letting go and living with a more peaceful state of mind.

# HOW CAN I LET GO?

## THE KEYS TO LETTING GO

### Accept your limits

The first thing to do is to accept the limits of reality and recognise your own limits. The former are defined by material limits: time, space, and so on; while the latter are psychological (am I patient? Do I have a particular gift for languages or maths?) and physical (am I healthy enough to run 100 metres?).

The second kind of limits are flexible to a certain extent, which is rarely the case with the external physical reality. We can illustrate this with a very simple example. If I want to cross a stream with no bridge without getting my feet wet, I only have two options: either I cross it and get wet, or do not cross it. If I get angry or frustrated, or if I stubbornly wait for the stream to dry up (which could take quite some time!), this means that I am refusing to accept the limits of reality. On the other hand, if I accept this physical reality, I can decide to walk alongside the stream until I find a dry part, or accept the unpleasantness of walking with wet feet and shoes, in the knowledge that they will dry in the end.

## CHANGE THE WAY YOU LOOK AT THE WORLD

Here is a little exercise to change how you look at things when you are in a bad mood.

First of all, get a piece of paper and write down everything that has been troubling you and putting you in a bad mood lately. When you have finished, close your eyes. Imagine that you are walking through a beautiful park on a glorious summer morning. The air is calm and you can hear birds singing. You can feel the morning dew and the gentle heat of the sun's rays as they shine down on your face, and you can smell roses and jasmine. As you are walking, you pass other walkers; they smile at you and you smile back. Everything about your walk is perfect.

When you feel ready, open your eyes. Go back to your piece of paper and see how your point of view on things has changed. If you want to, you can write down how you feel about your problems now and make a note of the changes.

Do the exercise again every time you are feeling down and reread your old notes. They will help you to put things into perspective and remind you of the incredible power of your mind.

This exercise will show you that it is possible to change the way you view things. No matter what your circumstances, your mind remains free. Becoming aware of this is very important and will help you in all situations in life.

Obviously, we cannot work on accepting our limits until we know about the world around us and, more specifically, about the factors in a problem. This means that small children cannot carry out this kind of work. When they cry or throw a tantrum, it is often because they do not understand why particular limits have been set for them. Often, a quick explanation will be enough to calm them down. For example, if you tell a 2-year-old not to touch a hot kettle without giving them any explanation, they will immediately start crying; on the other hand, if you tell them that they will burn themselves, they will find it easier to let go of the feeling of unfairness that was making them angry.

Similarly, an adult who is unsure about or does not understand a situation will find it more difficult to let go. It is therefore important to take the time to gather more information if you can. Talking, discussing things with your friends and going to therapy can also help you to become more aware of your limits and accept them more easily.

## Accept your emotions

We can generally control our feelings of frustration once we realise that they are useless, but it is more difficult to do this when dealing with emotionally charged events. For example, when we lose a loved one, the things we need to let go of are our will to overcome our grief and our desire to forget and move on too quickly. Indeed, many of us suppress our emotions instead of trying to control them. However, this can be harmful to our mental, and even our physical, health.

The things we are feeling are natural, and it would be unfair to repress them completely. It is better to observe them as an external object. This will help us to mitigate their effect, as we will no longer identify directly with them; in other words, we will lose the subconscious tendency to think that "I am my anger" or "I am my sadness". These emotions are only temporary and do not represent our true self, the person that we really are. We are the sum of all our emotions, experiences, ideals, and so on. Sometimes we are happy, sometimes we are sad; none of this lasts forever. If we embrace all our emotions and are understanding, forgiving and kind to ourselves, negative emotions will end up having less of a place in our lives.

Of course, it is not easy to take a step back from very difficult events. It is worth starting by accepting that we all face challenges, but we can also see these as an opportunity for change. We must remember that we can think differently, no matter how difficult the situation, and accept that there are no miracle solutions. However, there are some little things that can help us to get over our pain.

<u>**SOME TIPS FOR GETTING THROUGH**</u>
<u>**DIFFICULT SITUATIONS**</u>

To put distance between yourself and your negative thoughts when dealing with a difficult situation, try to:

- Avoid isolating yourself. It is important to stay in touch with other people, both loved ones and more casual acquaintances, and to communicate. Other people's help and empathy will strengthen your morale and self-esteem.
- Keep living normally (work, go shopping, maintain your social life). Holding on to little everyday things and telling yourself that each of these things is vital will make you feel better. It is essential to grant importance even to things that may seem trivial (going for a walk, looking out at the street, watching your child, and so on).

This will help your mind to calm down and drive out negative emotions by bringing your attention back to your feelings and to a less harsh reality.

If you cannot do this all the time and your

negative ideas come back, tell yourself that it is not a big deal. Accept your thoughts and keep in mind that they will eventually lessen and maybe even disappear.

## Observe your thoughts

It is very useful to become aware of the way we think and the content of our thoughts without identifying with them. This awareness will reveal a series of tendencies that are hidden within us and that harm us. These could include our tendency to:

- Constantly dwell on the past. As there is nothing we can do to bring it back, continually thinking about the past only feeds our bitterness and sadness. However, it is still possible to draw constructive conclusions from our past experiences.
- Fear failure. Fear of failure paralyses us, but if we embrace challenges, we can evolve and develop.
- Fear the future. Being afraid of things that may or may not happen in a more or less distant future will stop us from moving forward. Of

course, there will be unexpected things, but they are part of the beauty of life. It is much more constructive to recognise what we can really control and work on these things are well as we can.

- Worry about other people. Worrying about someone is not necessarily a sign of love, and worrying too much about one of your loved ones will not help them at all. Quite the opposite, in fact: they may end up lacking confidence in themselves and their abilities.
- Picking faults in ourselves. We all have our flaws, but the good news is that we all have good qualities too. Faults and qualities are what makes each individual interesting and valuable.

These thoughts, which can sometimes become obsessive, also stop us from seeing our good side. Some people tend to focus too much on the negatives, but looking at the positives is very helpful. We can also develop our qualities and work on our flaws. While we cannot change everything, we still have the power to influence many things: for example, we cannot change our age, but we can decide to get active and exercise to improve our health and feel younger. Even more simply, we can decide to accept our age with all the joys, pain and worries it brings.

# TECHNIQUES FOR LETTING GO

## Breathing

When we are worried, our breathing is generally short, rapid and shallow. We may even end up holding our breath. On the other hand, when we are calm and relaxed, our breathing tends to be deep and regular. Furthermore, many people only breathe from the top of their body (clavicular breathing), which is how we breathe when we feel threatened. Clavicular breathing is part of a sympathetic nervous system response that allows us to react in situations of threat or stress. In modern life, our sympathetic nervous system is called upon so much that it often ends up exhausting our body. In this case, the parasympathetic nervous system, which slows down our functions and calms us down by working against the sympathetic nervous system, is no longer able to restore our balance.

Clavicular breathing, like thoracic breathing,

therefore excites the nervous system. In clavicular breathing, as the name suggests, we breathe by raising our clavicles. Very anxious people who think constantly often breathe like this. In thoracic breathing, it is our ribs that move up and down. This kind of breathing also excites our nervous system, and is generally used inconsistently by angry or stressed people. However, its negative effects are less extreme than those of clavicular breathing.

In contrast to these kinds of breathing, which use the top of our torso and excite our nervous system, there is another type, known as diaphragmatic or deep breathing, which calms us down. Diaphragmatic breathing strengthens our parasympathetic nervous system.

Obviously, the ideal balance is to combine clavicular, thoracic and diaphragmatic breathing: this is known as complete breath. This technique allows blood and energy to circulate throughout the entire body so that it functions in a balanced, harmonious way.

You will see that mindset and breathing are closely linked. Yogis, Buddhist monks and Zen masters all use this principle of psychosomatic interaction to develop their meditation and breathing techniques, which help practitioners to let go and live better.

Breathing helps us to let go because it takes our mind off our thoughts to focus on the here and now, and then on pure breathing. The more the sensation is sharpened, the closer we will be to what these Eastern techniques call the Self (we could also call it the soul). In a way, it is the core of our being, stripped of our mental constructions and the conditioning we have undergone our entire lives.

To start with, observe everything that is happening around you and in your body, and also all the thoughts, whether simple or disruptive, that come into your head. You will then become conscious of your breathing and its simplicity. Keep in mind that this is a gentle process and you are not looking to achieve a particular goal.

The exercise of breathing can be very liberating and can help us to let go immediately. However, regular daily practice is the only way we can train our minds to do this with more and more ease.

**Breathing focused on a mental object**

When you experience a negative feeling (anger, obsession, sadness, and so on), focus on your breathing in order to lessen the intensity of the emotion.

The technique is simple:

- when you breathe out, exhale anger and sadness;
- when you breathe in, inhale joy, confidence and peace.

Repeat the exercise several times until you feel better.

**Simple breathing**

You can also focus on the air going in and out of your nostrils, gently and without forcing yourself, while sitting (either cross-legged on the floor, or on a chair) with your back straight or lying down. Take air in, let air out and, above all, take the time to feel the benefits!

## Alternate nostril breathing

You can also try the Yogic breathing technique known as *Nadi Shodhana* ("purification of the *nadis*", where the *nadis* are the energy channels identified by yogis which correspond roughly to our nervous and circulatory systems, also similar to the energy channels in Chinese medicine). It is very effective for calming, clearing and refreshing the mind. It should be fluid and natural.

Alternate nostril breathing is carried out with the help of a *mudra* (a precise, symbolic gesture for yogis) performed with the hands. During the exercise, the right hand should be used to block the nostrils; you need to open it, then fold your index and middle finger against your palm. Your thumb remains free and is used to block your right nostril. Your ring finger and little finger are used to block your left nostril. You will easily work out where to press on the outside of your nose to stop the passage of air. Your hand there-fore remains by your nose for the entire exercise. You will see that this gesture will soon seem natural to you.

The diagram below will help you to understand

the movements to carry out:

### Alternate nostril breathing

We can work through the
exercise together.

Go through the following
cycle around ten times.

**1.**

Breathe in through
your left nostril,
using your right
thumb to block your
right nostril.

**2.**

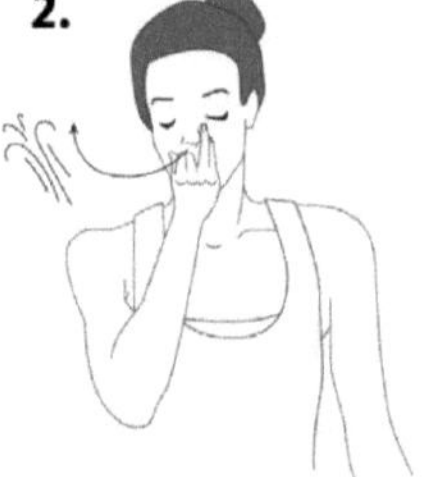

Breathe out through
your right nostril,
using the ring finger
and little finger of
your right hand to
block your left nostril.

Keeping your left
nostril blocked,
breathe in through
your right nostril.

Block your right
nostril and breathe
out though your
left nostril



> **A FEW QUICK TIPS**
>
> There is no point forcing your breathing. Breathe as naturally as you can. Gradually, you can start taking longer breaths. You will then notice a more and more profound effect and will experience inner calm.

## Abdominal breathing

You can also train yourself with diaphragmatic breathing (the diaphragm is the main breathing muscle). Abdominal breathing has a significant effect on all your muscles, nerves and organs, which means that it will calm your mind and strengthen you against stress. When practiced on a daily basis, it results in a positive mindset and drives out negative ideas.

Lie down, bend your knees while keeping your feet flat on the floor, and place one hand on your stomach. Breathe in, letting air gently enter your stomach, which will swell. Breathe out, gently contracting your stomach. Breathing out is more 'active' than breathing in. Above all, do not force anything; your breathing should remain as fluid and natural as possible.

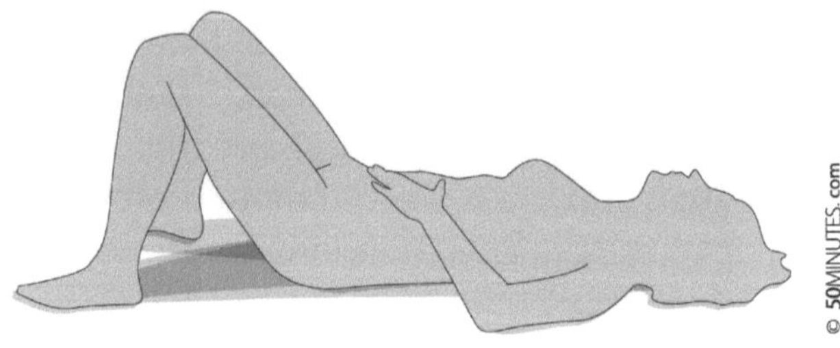


Ideally, you should practice this abdominal breathing before going to sleep. It will allow you to have a restful night.

# Relaxation

There are many relaxation techniques. Most of them will help you to let go, because they involve using relaxation to calm your thoughts and negative emotions.

For the two exercises below, lie down on your back or sit down, depending on what is most comfortable for you. Feel free to put a blanket over you for warmth, because relaxation decreases your body temperature.

## Relaxing by imaging yourself in a pleasant situation or recalling a happy memory

Lie on your back with your arms and legs slightly apart from your body and your palms facing upwards, or sit up with your back straight, and close your eyes. If you are lying down, feel all the points of contact between your body and the ground: heels, calves, thighs, buttocks, shoulder blades, upper arms, forearms, the back of your hands and the back of your head. If you are sitting down, feel the points of contact under your buttocks, at the lowest part of your pelvis. Once you are well anchored in your chair or on the floor, let relaxation wash over you and let go of your control over your body. Do not forget to relax your face and jaw, as we often tend to clench them when we are stressed.

Relax by thinking about a holiday or a good time with friends, or think about a place that means a lot to you, and remain in the setting your memory suggests to you. Remember all the sensations, whether they come from your sense of sight, sound, smell or even taste. Visualise yourself in the middle of these sensations. Feel as though you are in the place you are thinking of. Really take your time and make the most of your memory.

Your breathing should be deep, calm and regular.

Visualise yourself smiling and feel your smile flood your entire body. Let yourself be carried by this moment of peace and happiness.

## Visualising yourself free of a problem

In the same position as the previous exercise, imagine yourself free of a problem and visualise how you were able to overcome it, either simply, with a bit of effort or with some difficulty. Pay attention to the sensations that accompany your thoughts. You will see that some thoughts are pleasant, while others are more troublesome. You will see that you can be fair, forgiving and kind to yourself.

You can finish this relaxation exercise by visualising your breathing. Breathe naturally through your nose and gently let air into your relaxed body. A smile may even have spontaneously broken out on your face. You are happy and feel at peace with yourself.

However, do not use this technique if your problem is too serious and you cannot see a solution. In this case, you need help or more time to think things over. If you find yourself in this situation, you could remember old problems that you managed to solve or that resolved themselves. This will strengthen your confidence in life and in your own abilities.

## Meditation and mindfulness

Meditation involves observing and focusing your mind in order to calm down. Its immediate effect is to anchor us in the here and now. It therefore has nothing do to with daydreaming and is not really a form of relaxation, because it is largely active. You remain alert, but you are still relaxed.

For example, if you choose to sit on a chair or to sit with your legs crossed, make sure that your spine remains straight, without becoming tense. The rest of your body should be relaxed. This will help you stay awake and will encourage circulation between your brain and the base of your spine.

Meditation has existed for thousands of years and has been passed down by various spiritual doctrines. However, as modern science has recognised the benefits of these techniques, meditation has lost the spiritual connotation it had for many people. From a medical point of view, researchers have recently discovered not only that it has a beneficial effect on the body (it calms breathing, slows the heart rate, and so on), but also that it changes the structure of the brain by allowing the creation of new neuronal circuits. In addition, it strengthens our parasympathetic nervous system.

Meditation and mindfulness will help you to let go by calming your mind, visualising your worries with detachment and observing the way you think about and feel things. Like with breathing and relaxation, you will get better results with short daily (or at least frequent) sessions than with long occasional sessions.

## Seated meditation

Choose a calm place where nobody can disturb you and cover up so that you do not get cold: like relaxation, meditation decreases your body temperature.

Sit on a chair with your back straight, your hands on your thighs and your feet firmly planted on the floor, or sit cross-legged on a small cushion or folded towel with your hands on your knees and your palms facing upwards. Although your back should be straight, the rest of your body should be supple and relaxed. Whatever position you choose, make sure you are comfortable. You can have your eyes open or closed.

Start by paying attention to your posture and all of your sensations. Observe or, if your eyes are closed, visualise your environment. Listen to near or distant sounds and take in smells and the humidity or dryness of the air. Gradually pay attention to the thoughts that come to you. Observe them as if they were objects. See how they come and go. Observe these constant movements. Do not judge anything, but simply watch. When an emotion passes, note how it affects you and how you can also remain completely indifferent to it. Avoid tensing up and keep embracing your thoughts and feelings. If you feel the need, extend your meditation with a few breathing exercises. There may still be some feelings and thoughts to come. All you have to do is observe them and let them go afterwards. Stay relaxed. You can end your session with a short relaxation exercise.

## Day-to-day mindfulness

Psychologists and psychiatrists developed mindfulness as a treatment to provide their stressed, anxious patients with some relief. It takes up the main idea of Zen Buddhism, which it emerged directly from, namely to have the consciousness fully present in the here and now.

Mindfulness is in a way simpler and more fundamental, because it allows your mind to become aware of what you are currently experiencing or doing, at any point in your day-to-day life. It can therefore be practised anywhere and at any time, whatever you are doing and whatever the position of your body.

The idea of this exercise is to fully immerse yourself in what you are currently doing. To do this, you should use your senses and observe rather than judge. Thoughts will come to you, but you should not look for them.

Here is a non-exhaustive list of activities during which you can practise mindfulness:

- Walking. Focus on the contact of your feet with the ground, pay attention to your breathing and observe what you feel in your body.
- Washing and getting ready. Pay attention to the water as it touches your skin and the smoothness of the soap.
- Meals. Chew slowly and savour the flavours, tastes and textures of the food you are eating.
- Cooking. Cook simply, but appreciate every product you use and put your heart into what

you are doing, whether you are preparing food for yourself or for other people. Something as simple as chopping vegetables can be a very rewarding experience.

- Listening to other people. Listen closely to the other person and be as empathetic as possible; do not judge, observe what their words make you feel and let them pass.
- Playing with a child. Put yourself on their level and share their joy and laughter without over-thinking things.

## A few other ways of letting go

Water has both a real and a symbolic purifying function. It can help you to wash away your thoughts, whether by drinking it, taking a shower, going for a swim, trying thalassotherapy, and so on.

You should also regularly sort the things you no longer need, both at home and at work. If you are thinking too much about keeping a particular item, force yourself to get rid of it. Likewise, when you tell yourself that a particular object might come in useful one day, throw it out. You can donate, sell or recycle the things you no longer want. You will not lose anything; instead, you will increase your self-esteem, help others and do something good for the planet.

## A FEW FINAL TIPS

Taking care of yourself is essential! You cannot think straight when you do not feel well physically. Sleep as much as you need to feel good, eat healthily, stay active and breathe.

Make sure you also take care of others and nurture them, without suffocating them. Empathy is one of the best ways of healing your soul. It will help you to let go and put things into perspective much more easily.

# HOW CAN I STAY RELAXED AFTER LETTING GO?

Letting go is a continual task that requires a great deal of perseverance. Our minds will always tend to fixate on our thoughts and problems, but they will do this less if we work to develop reflexes that stop us from dwelling on things. You should start using the techniques outlined in this guide as soon as possible. In addition, you need to bear in mind that everyone is capable of changing their behaviour and their mindset.

Our brain's ability to adapt to new things is almost limitless, but it requires work and effort. In this way, it is a bit like our bodies: they need exercise to build muscle, and the stronger our muscles are, the easier exercise will be.

It is important to believe in and trust this approach, but do not expect too much. The key is to keep moving forward and stay confident.

# FAQS

## DOES EVERYONE FIND IT EQUALLY DIFFICULT TO LET GO?

No: everyone has their own personality, situation and life experiences. A more introverted person who is very occupied by their thoughts will find it harder to let go than someone who is more extroverted. The same goes for people who have a lot of worries or who experience difficult events, because they will struggle to put things in perspective.

Having said that, everyone can try letting go. Come out of your shell, talk to people, exchange your points of view and get your ideas out in the open. Putting things into perspective by looking at other people's opinions and the diversity of life will allow you to take a step back.

If you catch yourself shying away from the real issue, examine the new benefits you would be able to get from your life if you did not let your problems rule you.

Of course, it is not always easy to realise that your problems sometimes conceal other worries. Try to be as honest as possible with yourself and look at yourself as a friend. To do this, it is often useful to take a step back: go somewhere else, do something you do not usually do, meet other people or go on a retreat (to a calm place, to nature or with a spiritual group, for example).

You can also try talking about yourself in the third person, as if you were observing someone else. Be fair: make sure that you are not too lenient or too harsh towards yourself.

These different approaches and help from someone else will enable you to look at yourself, put things in perspective and find the root of the problem. Think about the fact that some people have the same problems, or even worse problems, than you, but they still look on the bright side and manage to be satisfied and happy with their lives. Be aware of this, but do not beat yourself up about it either.

## DO CHILDREN FIND IT EASIER TO LET GO?

Yes and no. Young children often fixate on what they want immediately, sometimes with impressive determination, and they can throw impressive tantrums if they do not get it. However, unlike us, they are also able to let go suddenly and completely of the thing they want and stop thinking about it altogether, either because something else has caught their attention or because they have been consoled.

When we reach adulthood, negative impressions tend to affect us more deeply and stay with us for a fairly long time. If we could let go of things immediately, we would never be bitter. You should therefore feel free to take inspiration from the psychological flexibility of children. Sometimes wanting to think about something else is all it takes to make it happen, and thinking like a child will allow us to constantly wonder at the world around us.

## WHAT MAKES IT DIFFICULT FOR US TO LET GO?

The reason it is difficult to let go of a thought or an emotion is that our mind prefers to think about things that occupy and preoccupy it. We like to spend our time observing a problem from all angles, when in fact it just keeps obsessing us while the solution continues to elude us. It is an addictive process, and we are the only ones who can decide to put an end to it.

It is important to get into the habit of telling yourself that you can move on to something else, as long as you do not start dwelling on other things, of course. The idea is to say "stop" and think about or do something else instead, because wanting to stop thinking about or run away from a problem will only make you more attached to it.

## TO WHAT EXTENT SHOULD WE LET GO?

A reluctance to let go is often linked to the fear of losing control. This is why it is important to be aware of your own capacities and external limits.

You should let go as much as is acceptable and comfortable for you, without harming other people and while acknowledging that you cannot make everyone happy or control other people's behaviour and reactions.

If you are tired and stressed because you are working too much, but work is very important to you, you can give yourself a few days off to relax, reminding yourself that you have the right to do this and it will not have negative consequences later on. If you have a demanding boss who does not look too kindly on your need for a break, you can ask yourself whether you might be better off working somewhere that will be more understanding of your needs and your private life.

Letting go may lead to the emergence of other problems, which is obviously not pleasant but can sometimes be necessary. It is up to you to see what you can leave behind and how far you can go, making sure to take into account what is really important for you.

# WHAT IS THE BEST WAY TO LET GO?

It is up to you to experiment with the different techniques suggested in this guide and find the ones that work for you. You need to look at the time you have available and the extent of your problems. If you think that you cannot manage it alone, feel free to get help by talking things over with your loved ones, taking relaxation classes or consulting a specialist.

Above all, keep things in proportion and have faith in life.

*We want to hear from you!*
*Leave a comment on your online library*
*and share your favourite books on social media!*

# FURTHER READING

## BIBLIOGRAPHY


- André, C. (2011) *Méditer jour après jour. 25 leçons pour vivre en pleine conscience.* Paris: L'Iconoclaste.

- Chödrön, P. (1997) *Entrer en amitié avec soi-même. Dire oui à soi-même, se réconcilier avec soi-même et le monde.* Paris: Pocket.

- Farcet, G. (2014) *Le choix d'être heureux.* Toulouse: UPPR.

- Jollien, A. (2012) *Petit traité de l'abandon. Pensées pour accueillir la vie telle qu'elle se propose.* Paris: Éditions Seuil.

- Van Lysbeth, A. (2007) *Pranayama: The Energetics of Breath.* New York: Harmony Books.

- Van Lysbeth, A. (2002) *Yoga Self-Taught.* Varanasi: Pilgrims Publishing.

- Nhat Hanh, (2010) *You Are Here: Discovering the Magic of the Present Moment.* Boulder, Colorado: Shambhala Publications.

- Nhat Hanh, T. (2008) *The Miracle of Mindfulness.* London: Rider.

- Ricard, M. (2015) *Happiness: A Guide to Developing Life's Most Important Skill.* New York: Little, Brown and Company.

- De Smedt, M. (1983) *Techniques de méditation et pratiques d'éveil*. Paris: Éditions Albin Michel.

- Suzuki, S. (1973) *Zen Mind, Beginner's Mind*. Boston, Massachusetts: Shambhala Publications, Inc.

- Townsend, I. (1997) *Yoga anti-stress*. Paris: Éditions Marabout.

- Vigne, J. (2007) *Soigner son âme, méditation et psychologie*. Paris: Éditions Albin Michel.

## ADDITIONAL SOURCES

- Collard, P. (2014) *The Little Book of Mindfulness: 10 Minutes a Day to Less Stress, More Peace*. London: Gaia Books.

- Williams, M. and Penman, D. (2011) *Mindfulness: A Practical Guide to Finding Peace in a Frantic World*. London: Piaktus.

Although the editor makes every effort to verify the accuracy of the information published, 50Minutes.com accepts no responsibility for the content of this book.



www.50minutes.com

Ebook EAN: 9782808000581

Paperback EAN: 9782808000598

Legal Deposit: D/2017/12603/457

Cover: © Primento

Digital conception by Primento, the digital partner of publishers.